This Book Belongs to :

Isaac, Isabel + Ilise
McGraw
Happy Easter !
Love, Auntie & Uncle
Lynn + Todd
1999

Published in Nashville, Tennessee, by Tommy Nelson™, a division of Thomas Nelson, Inc.

Scripture quotations are from the *International Children's Bible, New Century Version*, copyright © 1986 by Word Publishing. Used by permission.

To contact the author, please write: Liz Curtis Higgs
                                                P.O. Box 43577
                                                Louisville, KY 40253-0577

Library of Congress Cataloging-in-Publication Data

Higgs, Liz Curtis
    The parable of the lily/by Liz Curtis Higgs; illustrated by Nancy Munger.
        p. cm.
        Summary: A farmer's daughter receives a mysterious gift which she neglects and then discards, only to find out on Easter morning how special it is. Bible verses link the story to the life of Jesus.
    ISBN 0-7852-7231-3
    [1. Parables. 2. Lilies-Fiction. Easter-Fiction.] I. Munger, Nancy, ill. II. Title.
PZ7.H543955Par 1997
[E]-dc20   96-44222
                                                               CIP
                                                               AC

Printed in the United States of America

99 00 01 02 03 QPH 9 8 7 6 5 4

The Parable of the Lily

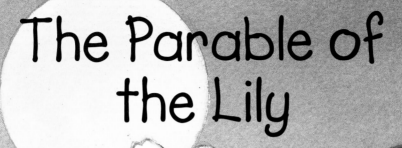

by
Liz Curtis Higgs

Illustrated by Nancy Munger

Tommy
NELSON

Thomas Nelson Publishers
Nashville • London • Vancouver

For Lillian Margaret Higgs,
our own Easter lily

One wintry day the Farmer's young daughter shuffled through the snow, headed for the mailbox at the end of the lane. B-r-r-r, it was cold!

She peered inside the mailbox and found a small white envelope. Surprise! It was addressed to her!

"Dear Maggie," the letter began. "I'm sending a very special gift just for you. Look for it soon!"

Maggie loved getting presents, especially a gift as mysterious as this one. When would it come? Who was it from? What would it be?

"Every perfect gift is from God."
James 1:17

The Farmer's daughter waited and waited . . . some days patiently, some days not so patiently. Then one very ordinary afternoon, a box appeared on her doorstep. The gift had arrived!

The Farmer watched as His daughter excitedly tore off the wrapping paper. He was eager to see what she thought of her present.

But Maggie didn't say a word. She just stared at the small wooden crate full of dirt. Dirt was not at all what Maggie had hoped for!

"There was nothing in his appearance to make us desire him." Isaiah 53:2d

Poking out of the soil was a small piece of paper that told Maggie how to care for her gift.

Hide in a cool dark place

Water as needed

When spring comes bring into the light

Then she knew it must be a growing thing, like a bulb that would some day bloom into a plant.

LIVE PLANTS

"He grew up like a small plant before the Lord. He was like a root growing in a dry land." Isaiah 53:2a,b

Oh dear. Her long-awaited gift wasn't a toy or a doll or a game after all.

The Farmer could see that His daughter was very disappointed. His heart grew sad. The gift was from Him.

"For God loved the world so much that he gave his only Son." John 3:16

With a sigh, Maggie carried the wooden box down the steps into the darkest corner of the cellar and left it there on a shelf.

Sometimes she remembered to water it, but most of the time, Maggie just plain forgot.

"He had no special beauty or form to make us notice him." Isaiah 53:2c

The Farmer
did not forget.
He just waited.
And He watched.

"Wait until the Lord comes.
He will bring to light
things that are now hidden in darkness."
1 Corinthians 4:5

Spring came at last.
The air was warmer, and the gray skies had melted into robin's egg blue. What a welcome sight the sun was!

It was time for the Farmer to hoe His garden, getting the soil ready for the seeds that filled His pockets.

"In the same way the Lord God will make grow what is right." Isaiah 61:11

Maggie wanted to help,
    so she marched down
        the cellar steps to get
            her own Maggie-size
                gardening tools.
                    That's when
                        it happened.

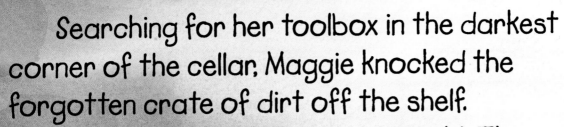

Searching for her toolbox in the darkest corner of the cellar, Maggie knocked the forgotten crate of dirt off the shelf.

Crash! The crate splintered into pieces, soil was everywhere, and the flower bulb that rolled to her feet showed no signs of life.

"I tell you the truth. A [seed] must fall to the ground and die. Then it makes many seeds." John 12:24

What a mess! Maggie was mad at the box and even madder at herself. She swept up the dirt and threw away the broken box, grumbling under her breath.

"He was hated and rejected by people. ... People would not even look at him." Isaiah 53:3

And that ugly old flower bulb?
She tossed it out the cellar door,
never to think of it again.

Until...

Maggie woke up earlier than usual Easter morning. A warm breeze blew through her bedroom window, and the chirping birds seemed to call her name.

Still dressed in her nightgown, Maggie tiptoed out into the garden. She was hoping to find some daffodils or tulips to decorate the table for Easter breakfast.

That's when she saw it. The loveliest lily that God ever made was blooming on the edge of her Father's flower garden.

"Thanks be to God for his gift that is too wonderful to explain."
2 Corinthians 9:15

Its white petals unfolded like a trumpet.
Its leaves were green with new life. Its scent
was as fragrant as the most expensive perfume.

*"But I tell you that even Solomon with his riches
was not dressed as beautifully
as one of these flowers." Matthew 6:29*

Maggie knew all at once what had happened.
She didn't know whether to laugh or cry or
shout with joy. So Maggie did all three at once.
"Wake up, everybody! Wake up! Come see!
The gift is alive!"

*"They were afraid, but they were also very happy.
They ran to tell … what had happened."* Matthew 28:8

Her family hurried out to the garden. They couldn't believe their eyes! So much beauty from such an ugly box of dirt.

"Your eyes will see the king in his beauty." Isaiah 33:17

Maggie noticed the Farmer, standing in the doorway, quietly watching. His smile gave away His secret.

"Father, it was You who gave me the lily!" Maggie squealed with delight.

Suddenly her little girl smile began to fade.

Oh dear.

She'd thrown away her Father's gift without so much as a "thank you." How that must have hurt Him!

"But he took our suffering on him and felt our pain for us." Isaiah 53:4

"I'm sorry, Daddy," she said, putting her little arms around His big waist. "Will You forgive me?"

"Oh, My child," the Farmer whispered, hugging her tight. "That's what Easter is all about."

"This is how God showed his love to us:
He sent his only Son into the world
to give us life through him." 1 John 4:9